T5-CVF-892

Learning With ABC's

FRUITS and VEGETABLES

to Grow On

by

Doris Cambruzzi and Claire Thornton

illustrations by Lorraine Arthur

STANDARD PUBLISHING
Cincinnati, Ohio   3607

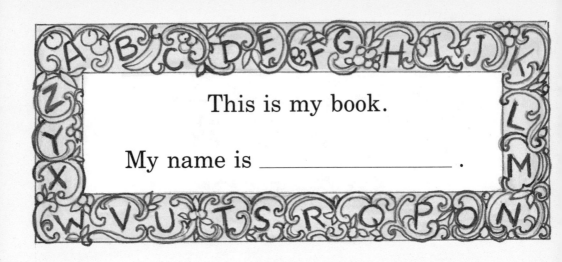

This is my book.

My name is _____ .

Library of Congress Catalog Card Number 86-060737
ISBN 0-87403-127-3

© 1986, The STANDARD PUBLISHING Company
Division of STANDEX INTERNATIONAL Corporation
Printed in U.S.A.

Dear Parent:

God, our loving Father, has entrusted our children to us, to guide and direct in both spiritual and bodily growth here on earth. This book is designed to help your children become familiar with good nutrition so that they will eat the correct foods for a healthy body.

Nutrition pertains to what we eat and how our bodies use it. Essential nutrients must be obtained from the foods we eat. Protein, carbohydrates, fat, vitamins, minerals, and water are the six classes of essential nutrients we obtain from our diets.

Whether we eat at home or we eat out, we are faced with important food choices. Children's needs change with age. One set of rules simply cannot apply to everyone. There is a practical guide to good nutrition, which translates the technical knowledge of nutrition into a plan for everyday eating. This guide, "The Four Food Groups," provides the kind and quantity of food necessary for a balanced diet. The Four Food Groups are Fruit-Vegetable Group, Meat Group, Milk Group, and Bread-Cereal Group.

A key to good health is to eat a variety of foods from each of the four food groups every day and get proper rest and exercise. It is very important to start your young children with good health habits.

Why do some people accept some foods and reject others? A primary factor in food acceptance seems to be the training of the young child in familiarity with a wide variety of foods. This training should be started at an early age, supported both in the home and by effective educational experiences.

Coauthor Doris Cambruzzi conducted a study on this subject and found that education, in addition to the provision of food, was an important factor in the vegetable consumption practices of children. The pattern of eating established during early childhood is believed to affect food choice and, to some extent, nutritional status throughout life. Assessments of the adequacy of the pre-schooler's diet have shown that vitamin A (retinol) and vitamin C (ascorbic acid) are two nutrients available often in less than the recommended amounts for children in this age group.

This book is a learning aid to help your child become familiar with fresh fruits and vegetables and to understand the correct portion that is needed by the body, which is the key to weight control throughout life. The realistic illustrations of fruits and vegetables contained in this book will help children identify them when shopping, and the recipes are easy and fun. Enjoy fresh fruits and vegetables. Enjoy a taste of good health!

—Doris Cambruzzi
—Claire Thornton

EAT A VARIETY OF FOODS FROM

MILK GROUP

Drink or eat 2 to 3 servings daily of foods from the Milk Group if you are under age 9. This group is a primary source of calcium. It also gives us phosphorous, riboflavin (vitamin B_2), and complete protein.

One serving from the
Milk Group

= 1 cup (8 ounces) of milk
= 1½ ounces of cheese
= 1¾ cups of ice cream
= 2 cups of cottage cheese
= 1 cup of yogurt

MEAT GROUP

Eat 2 or more servings daily of foods from the Meat Group. Foods in this group supply protein and iron and are a good source of the B vitamins.

One serving from the
Meat Group

= 2 or 3 ounces of cooked
  meat, poultry, or fish
= 2 eggs
= 1 cup of dry beans, peas,
  or lentils, cooked
= 4 tablespoons of peanut butter

THE FOUR FOOD GROUPS!

**BREAD-CEREAL
GROUP**

Eat 4 or more servings each day from the Bread-Cereal Group. Foods in this group supply many of the vitamins in the B complex, iron, carbohydrates, and limited amounts of protein. Fiber is present in whole grains.

One serving from the
Bread-Cereal Group

= 1 slice of bread
= 1 ounce of ready-to-eat cereal
= ½ to ¾ cup of cooked
    cereal, macaroni, rice,
    grits, or spaghetti

**FRUIT-VEGETABLE
GROUP**

Turn the page and have fun with the Fruit-Vegetable Group.

God made us, and God made the food we eat. God made the land and the sea, the sun and the moon, the rain and the air around us, and all the animals and plants for us to enjoy.

Fruits and vegetables are some of the foods that God gave us to eat. They taste good and are good for us.

God wants us to have healthy bodies and to take good care of our bodies. When we eat the right foods, we grow and feel good; and when we feel good, we can serve Him better.

This book tells you about fruits and vegetables, from A to Z. It shows you what they look like and gives you some recipes so that you can enjoy eating them in different ways. Some of them are good raw, some are good cooked, and some can be eaten either raw or cooked, whichever way you like them best.

Have fun eating fresh fruits and vegetables; they will help you stay healthy!

Fruits and Vegetables

Foods in this group are counted on to supply most of your daily needs of ascorbic acid (vitamin C) and retinol (vitamin A). Iron, potassium, folacin, and B_6 are also found in this group. Fiber is present in all vegetables.

Eat 4 or more servings each day. Include 1 serving of citrus and 1 serving of dark green or deep yellow vegetables and 2 servings of other fruits and vegetables including potatoes.

One serving is ½ cup of a vegetable or a fruit or a portion as ordinarily served, such as one medium banana.

Aa

Apple

Apricot

Artichoke

Avocado

Asparagus

Dressed-Up Apple Slices

Wash one large apple.
Core the apple.
Cut the apple into thin slices.
Spread each slice with peanut butter.
Enjoy!

Bb

Banana

Beans

Blueberries

Beets

Broccoli

Brussels
sprouts

Banana Nutra-Shake

½ cup skim milk
¼ banana, peeled
3 tablespoons orange juice concentrate
7 ice cubes

Put all of the ingredients in a
blender and whip until smooth.
Yields 1¾ cups.

Note: Other fruits may be used
in place of the banana.

Frozen Banana-Pops With Nuts

6 bananas
½ small can (3 ounces) frozen orange juice concentrate
¾ cup finely chopped nuts (almonds, walnuts, or pea-
   nuts)

Peel bananas and place on a cookie sheet covered with
wax paper.
Coat each banana with 1 tablespoon frozen orange
juice concentrate.
Place in freezer to chill (about 15 minutes).
Roll each banana in 2 tablespoons
chopped nuts, pressing in to coat.
Set in freezer until firm.
Serve frozen.

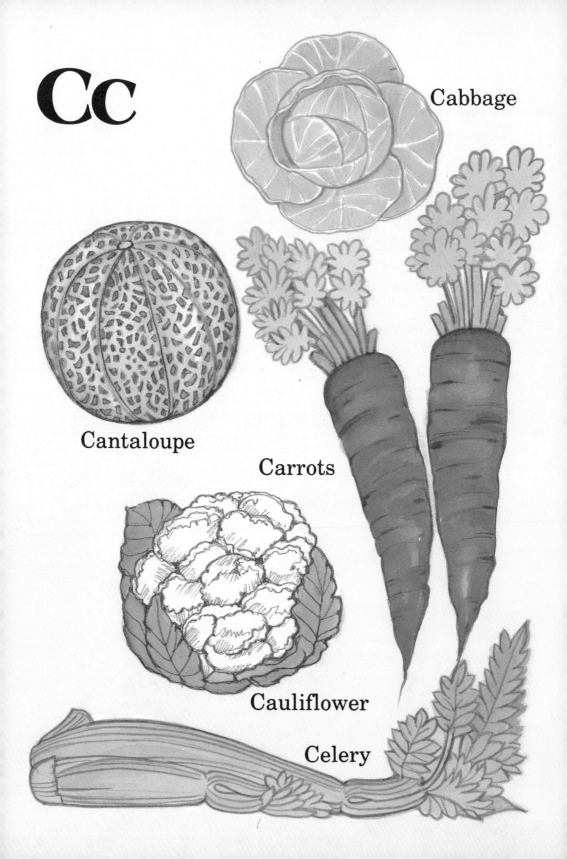

Cc

Cabbage

Cantaloupe

Carrots

Cauliflower

Celery

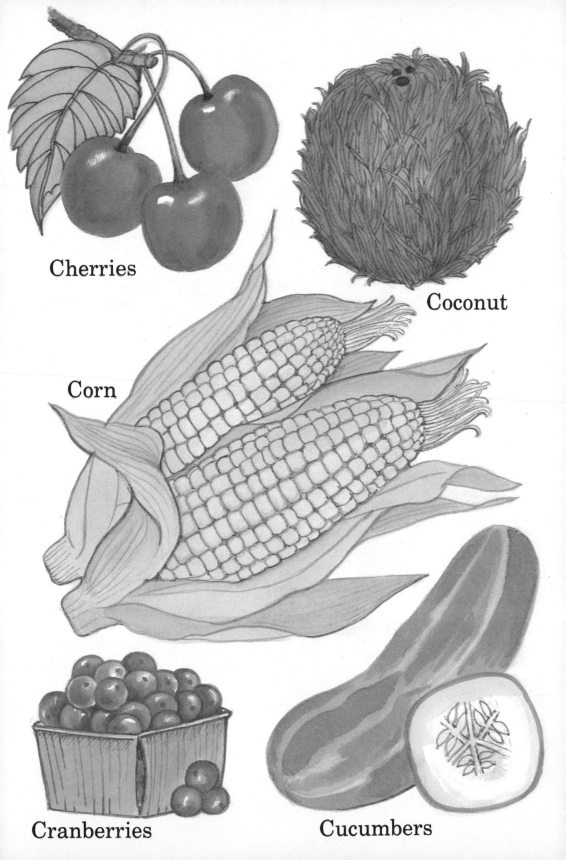

Cherries

Coconut

Corn

Cranberries

Cucumbers

Dd

Dandelion
greens

Dates

Holiday Stuffed Dates

1 box dates (pitted)
½ cup English walnuts (large pieces)
½ cup sugar

Place sugar in shallow bowl.
Place a walnut piece in each date where the pit was.
Press date around nut with fingers.
Roll in sugar.

Ee

Eggplant

Endive and Escarole

Ff Fruit

What is a fruit?

Fruit is the good-to-eat part that covers the seeds of flowering plants, trees, vines, and bushes.

Some fruits, like bananas and pineapples, are grown in tropical countries. Some fruits, like oranges and lemons, are grown in subtropical weather. And some fruits, like grapes, apples, pears, and berries, grow in temperate climates.

Fresh Fruit Treats

1 banana, cut up into bite-size pieces

1 orange, peeled and divided into sections

8 strawberries, washed well and patted dry with a paper
  towel

8 seedless grapes, washed and patted dry with a paper
  towel

8 fresh pineapple chunks

½ cup orange juice

Toothpicks

Garnishes:

¼ cup granola

¼ cup shredded coconut

¼ cup peanut bits

¼ cup toasted wheat germ

> Put garnishes on small plates.
> Pour orange juice into a bowl.
> Dip fruit in juice.
> Roll fruit to cover in one or all of the garnishes.
> Serve on plate with toothpicks.

Gg

Garlic

Grapefruit

Grapes

red

green

Green onions

Greens

collard

turnip tops

Satellite Balls

1 grapefruit
Pineapple chunks, grapes, cheese cubes, and/or raisins
Toothpicks

Select a grapefruit.

Stick toothpicks into one or more of the following: Pineapple chunks, grapes, cheese cubes, and raisins.

Then stick the toothpicks into the grapefruit.

Party Grapefruit

1 grapefruit
2 tablespoons
  brown sugar
2 cherries

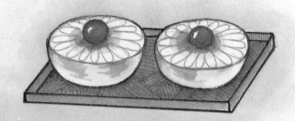

Cut grapefruit in half between ends so that the inside top of the grapefruit looks like spokes of a wheel.

Sprinkle each half with 1 tablespoon of brown sugar and put a red cherry in the middle.

Place on a cookie sheet 6 inches below a preheated broiler.

Broil for 3 minutes or until sugar is bubbly.

Serves 2.

Hh

Honeydew

Ii

Ice-Cream
fruit sundaes

Jj

Cranberry-Orange Jam

4 cups cranberries
2 cups water
Grated rind of 1 orange
1½ cups honey

Wash cranberries.

Combine with water and orange rind and boil for 10 minutes.

Puree in a blender and return to boil.

Add honey and boil gently for 10 minutes.

Pour into sterilized jelly jars and seal.

Makes 4 half-pint jars.

Refrigerate for safekeeping.

Kk

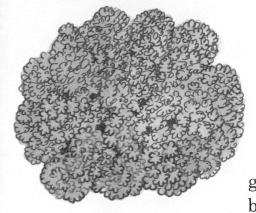

Kale

Kale leaves are grayish-blue to green and quite curly. They can be cooked like spinach. Kale also makes a pretty decoration for a party platter.

What is brown and fuzzy on the outside, emerald green on the inside? Kiwi fruit. Peel and eat, or cut in half and spoon it out of the skin. There are no seeds, no waste, and it's full of vitamin C.

Ripen at room temperature. Kiwi fruit gives to gentle palm pressure when ripe.

Kiwi

Kumquats

Kumquats are tiny orange citrus fruits that you can eat whole. The skin is sweet, the inside is sweet-tart. Wash well, then eat it in two little bites or one big bite.

Kumquats sliced in half, lengthwise, and spread with cream cheese make a good snack.

Ll

Lemons

Lettuce Roll-Ups

4 lettuce leaves
4 thin slices of ham
4 thin slices of cheese
Mustard
Toothpicks

Core and rinse one head of iceberg lettuce.
Select 4 crisp outer leaves.
Layer each lettuce leaf with one slice of ham, mustard to taste, and one slice of cheese.
Roll the lettuce sandwich up, jelly-roll style, fasten with a toothpick, and arrange the lettuce roll-ups on a platter to serve 4.

Limes

Lettuce

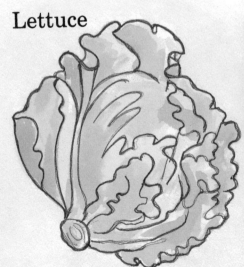

Mangoes

Mm

Mushrooms

Nn

A nectarine has tender, smooth skin that makes it good to eat. It contains vitamins A and C. Nectarines are sweet and juicy with a pit like a peach. They are available from spring to fall. Ripen them at room temperature for a day or two; when they yield to gentle palm pressure, they are ready to eat.

Nectarines

Dressed-Up Cheesecake

1 frozen cheesecake
3 medium-size nectarines, washed
¼ cup brown sugar

Thinly slice nectarines* (no peeling necessary).
Arrange on top of cheesecake.
Sprinkle with brown sugar.
Serves 6.

*To prevent discoloration of nectarine slices, dip or sprinkle with citrus juice.

Oo

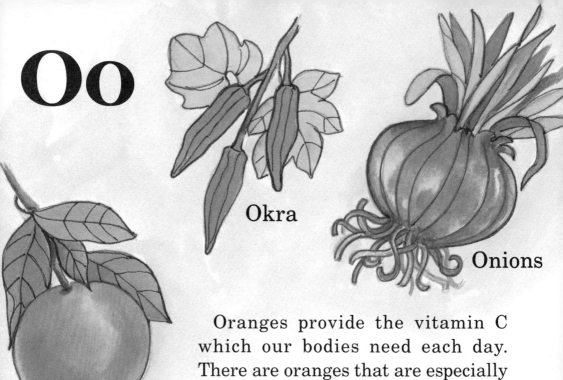

Okra

Onions

Oranges

Oranges provide the vitamin C which our bodies need each day. There are oranges that are especially good for making orange juice, like Valencia oranges. Navel oranges are good for snacks because they peel and separate into sections easily, and they have no seeds.

Dippy Oranges

1 navel orange, peeled and separated into sections

Yogurt Dip
½ cup plain yogurt
1 teaspoon honey
1 tablespoon orange juice

Mix together yogurt, honey, and orange juice.

Dip orange sections in yogurt mixture.

Yummy!

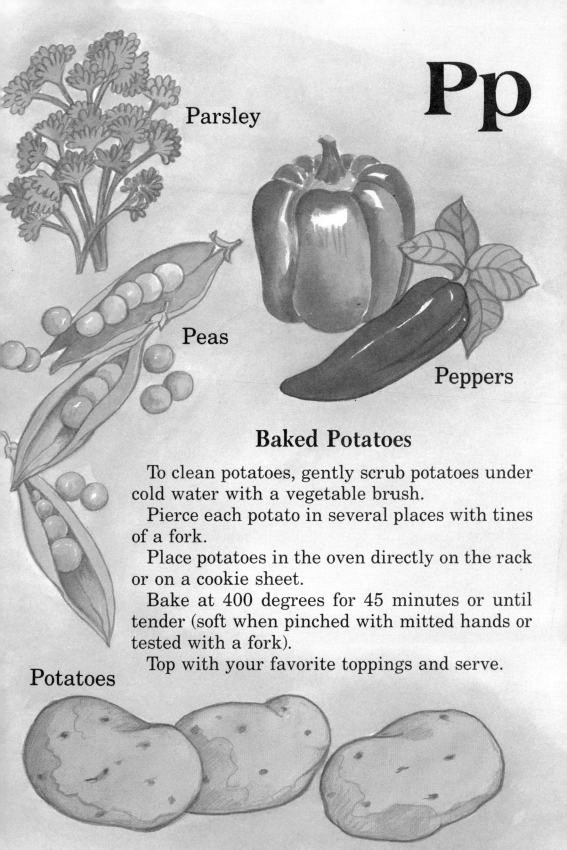

Pp

Parsley

Peas

Peppers

Baked Potatoes

To clean potatoes, gently scrub potatoes under cold water with a vegetable brush.

Pierce each potato in several places with tines of a fork.

Place potatoes in the oven directly on the rack or on a cookie sheet.

Bake at 400 degrees for 45 minutes or until tender (soft when pinched with mitted hands or tested with a fork).

Top with your favorite toppings and serve.

Potatoes

Papaya

Pumpkin

Peaches

Pears

Peach Shortcake

4 large peaches
¼ cup sugar
1 tablespoon lemon juice
1 pound cake or 4 small round sponge cakes
Whipped cream, optional

Peel and slice peaches.
Toss with sugar and lemon juice.
Slice pound cake.
Spoon peaches over pieces of cake.
Top with whipped cream if desired.
Serves 4.

Pineapple

Qq

The quince is related to the apple and the pear. It is used to make marmalade, jelly, and preserves.

Quince

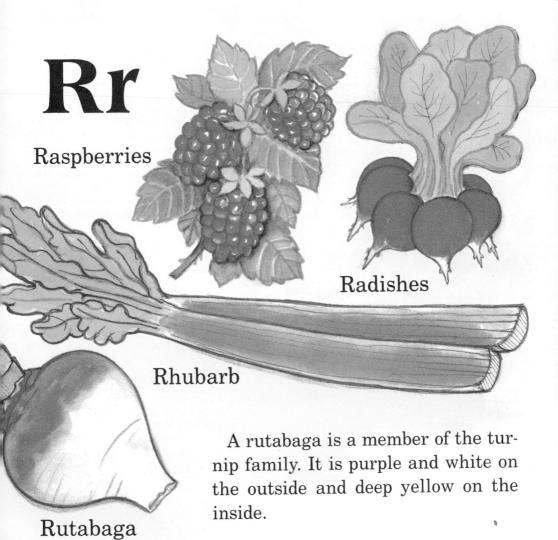

Rr

Raspberries

Radishes

Rhubarb

A rutabaga is a member of the turnip family. It is purple and white on the outside and deep yellow on the inside.

Rutabaga

Ss

Spinach

Swiss Chard

Squash

Butternut

Acorn

Spaghetti

Strawberries

Creamy Strawberry Shake

1 cup milk
1 tablespoon nonfat dry milk powder
1 cup strawberries (or other fruit)
2 teaspoons honey
½ cup creamed cottage cheese

Puree in a blender.
Makes 2 servings, each furnishing
13 grams of protein.
Serve with straw and garnish with
strawberry.

Tt

Tangelos

Tangelos are easy to peel; they are a combination of a tangerine and a grapefruit.

Tangerines

Tangerines are easy to peel and section. They are called a "zipper-skin" fruit.

Temple oranges

Temple oranges are fairly easy to peel, have a special orange flavor, and are available in January and February.

Tomatoes

Uu

Understand the difference between fruits and vegetables.

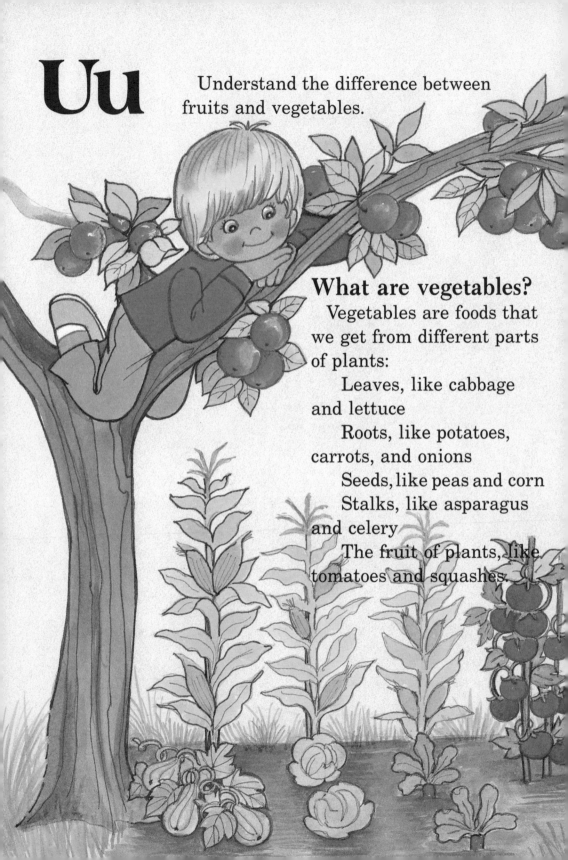

What are vegetables?

Vegetables are foods that we get from different parts of plants:

Leaves, like cabbage and lettuce

Roots, like potatoes, carrots, and onions

Seeds, like peas and corn

Stalks, like asparagus and celery

The fruit of plants, like tomatoes and squashes

Vegetable Kabobs

Cherry tomatoes
Carrot slices or curls
Green pepper squares
Rutabaga triangles
Turnip slices
Cucumber rings
Celery slices
Toothpicks or
shish kabob skewers

Select a variety of fresh vegetables.
String on toothpicks or skewers.

Vegetable

Watermelon

X-out foods low in nutri-
ents, and use fresh fruits
and vegetables for snacks.

Yy

Yams, or sweet potatoes, are low in calories and high in nutrients. They are a good source of vitamins A and C and also contain B_6, iron, potassium, and fiber.

Yams

Zz

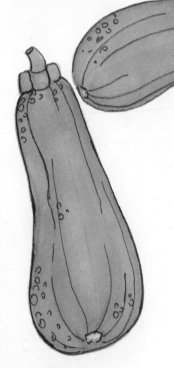

Zucchini

Veggie Wedgies

1 zucchini	1 carrot
2 celery stalks	1 small green pepper

Wash the vegetables well and cut into small sticks. Dip vegetables into cottage cheese mix.

Cottage Cheese Mix

Mix together in a bowl: 1 cup cottage cheese and 3 tablespoons cream cheese.

Add to bowl and blend together: 2 tablespoons yogurt and 2 tablespoons milk.

Add and blend: 1/8 teaspoon garlic salt, 1 dash pepper and 1½ tablespoons chopped chives.